What others are saying about Don't Laugh – A Woman's Playbook to the U-R-In Line for the Women's Public Bathroom…Again!

"To truly know something, one needs to experience it and the authors of this book really do know what they're talking about, as will most if not all women who read it. Funny and fully relatable, its down-to-earth contents describe an all too familiar experience and confirms why it should always be female architects who design women's public washrooms." *Gisele Jubinville, Healer with The Message Art*

"*Don't Laugh* is a hilarious read that every woman can relate to. I read it in one sitting and I kept thinking it was the perfect book for reading in the bathroom itself. Yes, I have often wondered why all women's bathrooms have long lines while men's do not; why more establishments don't repair broken locks and seats, ensure there's actually toilet paper available as well as paper towels or working dryers. The authors go into all these situations and much more. My only hope is the suggestions for the perfect ladies' bathroom is heeded by all public establishments. It would make life so much sweeter!" *International, Multi-Award-Winning Author P.M. Terrell*

"This amazing little book captures the private and public thoughts of women waiting In-Line for a Women's Public Bathroom. It will make you laugh out loud!" *Diane Albano Ed.D., Owner of LEAD Consulting and Coaching and Author of Nice Has No Voice Self-leadership Strategies*

"*Don't Laugh* offers a lighthearted way of changing the world, one pee at a time. I'm not sure if this book should be shelved with humour or community-building titles. Actually, it should just be left in public bathrooms across the country as a call-to-action and compassion for women of all bladder sizes." *Donna Barker, Award-winning Author and founder of Write, Woman, Write!*

Laugh it is the best medicine

(signature)

DON'T LAUGH

A Woman's Playbook to the U-R-In Line for the Women's Public Bathroom... Again!

By

Alisa Gamblin

Glenna Mageau

Helen Dougherty

May you Find the Humor in Life AGamblin

First Edition: Published 2017

©Copyright Alisa Gamblin, Glenna Mageau, Helen Dougherty (2017)

Published by: AGH Press 2017

Formatting: Patricia Terrell (P.I.S.C.E.S. Books)

Cover and Cover Art: Christine White

ISBN: 9780991727292

I gotta pee
I search high and low
Where the hell is the women's bathroom?
There it is and oh a lineup
What a shock
But what are the options.
Time is running out.

In line I stand
Waiting my turn
Maybe I should have come sooner
Can I hold it?
Did I really need that last sip of water?

My mind is consumed
Relieve this pressure
Tighten those muscles, hold on
Try to ease the pressure
But don't let anything go.

No laughing allowed
The infrastructure is too delicate
The muscles too tightly wound
Doing all they can
To stop the flow
That tells me I gotta go.

My bladder is stretching
Each second increases the pressure tenfold
I pray those Kegels I did 30 years before will hold
back the rush
Squeezing tight, I focus ahead
And do the slow in line shuffle forward.

Are we there yet?
My bladder tells me no
I try to look normal
With my insides anything but
They are primed and ready to let go.

I gotta pee
I gotta pee
Did you hear me
I gotta pee!
A line up is not what I'm looking for
A nice comfortable, fresh smelling toilet is what I
need
Now… thank you.

Please...

Introduction

Changing the world one pee at a time.

Have you ever wondered how much fun it is to stand in a lineup? Now imagine if you have to go pee? If you're a woman and you are at a public event, odds are you've been there... in line I mean... for a long time. Right? It is no fun to be in a lineup but just imagine your bladder is stretched to the limit begging you for relief and you just have to keep saying, 'just a few more minutes… I hope'. And then you wait… shuffle a bit forward and wait… shuffle a bit forward and wait… praying that your bladder will hold up... hoping women will move a little faster… hoping that there is a miracle and more bathrooms will show up immediately... You may also start wishing you hadn't had that last drink or that you lined up sooner or that you hadn't even gone to the event because you've spent all of your time in the lineup to the bathroom.

Your mind is consumed with getting to the front of the lineup, making it to a stall and getting your clothes off, well the necessary ones, so you can relieve this pressure that is building. That is when you become aware of how tiny the stall is. You have to back in, there is hardly room for you to fit and there is no place to hang your purse/bag. So you struggle with your belongings as you try to pull down your pants or lift your skirt so you can sit down and finally go. OMG you HAVE TO PEE… With relief you sit and ahhhhhh, thank god you made it. But then… oh no, there is no toilet paper. How did you not notice? Oh please let me have a Kleenex or something to wipe with. You wish you carried a roll of toilet paper in your purse/bag for times like this.

Men wonder why women have large purses/bags and carry so many things. This is one great reason why.

Another scenario is you finally find the women's bathroom only to see that dreaded sign, closed for cleaning. WHAT! Nooooooo. You have to go. Where is another bathroom? How far away is it? Can you make it? Why do they have to close the bathroom you want, can't they clean it later?

Now as much as we'd like to think all bathrooms are created equal, they aren't, especially public bathrooms. Some public bathrooms (many malls get this right), they are immaculate, classy, have the toilets to one side with plenty of space with the sinks kind of separate so there is room to enter and exit without women having to bump into or excuse themselves. And then... there are some public bathrooms where the toilet is in a tiny stall, and there aren't nearly enough for the number of women going through. They are so crowded that getting in and out is a chore. And washing your hands? Well that's a whole other problem. You are often right in the midst of the two lineups—the one squeezing past the lineup trying to get in and the one squeezing past trying to get out.

Anyway with the job complete, you are grateful that the bathroom has a toilet and not just a hole in the floor like you have heard about in some countries around the world. Can you imagine trying to hold your clothes up as you pull them down all just to hope you hit the hole in the floor and do not spray yourself? You realize you really should be feeling grateful for the toilets you have.

Having said all of that, we, as women, are very grateful for women's public bathrooms. Thank you to all of the places that offer them because without them there would be a whole lot more accidents.

So why are we telling you all of this? Why do we care if you stand in another lineup?

This is our light-hearted way of helping to change the world. Our goal is to bring smiles to faces, to help women get through that trying time, and shed some light on the topic of too few public bathrooms for women.

Why do we not look at the others and start up a conversation while we wait in line? Because WE HAVE TO PEE. Our entire attention is on forcing closed all of those muscles that we wish we had built up to hold this ever-expanding bladder. The more we focus on how bad we have to go the worse it gets.

We want to change that. We want you to have fun when in line and to get to know your neighbor, after all you could be hanging out together for a lot longer than you think. Besides chatting with someone will distract you. And if you talk to your neighbor in line, you'll realize we all have similar challenges. We're all not made the same but we do go through a lot of the same things.

This will also bring attention to the fact that there are many public venues that hold events and they do not even have close to the number of bathrooms that women need. Someday they may understand that when you keep a woman happy she will tell others. When you piss a woman off (pun intended), she will tell others.

Ladies we do have a voice, one that we can use in a pleasant way to let others know how we truly feel about long lineups… enough is enough.

And men please stay out of the women's line ups for bathrooms (it happens at too many outdoor events). Our lineups are full and we wait long enough as it is. And truly, we're tired of the wait… again!

Today… U-R-In line for the women's public bathroom…

Tomorrow… enough women's public bathrooms for all women… there is hope!

Smile, it just might make the difference in that long line up you find yourself in again.

Let's have some fun, life gives us enough stress without adding to it.

Chapter 1

Where the hell is the women's bathroom?

A question every woman ponders. Upon entering any establishment, the first thing most women will almost always do, is look around to discover where the closest bathroom is.

Why do you suppose we do that? Could it be that we know there is a very good chance that we will have to wait in line to use it so we want a head start on where it is located? After all when attending a big event, being the first in line to use the bathroom is key to prevent that strained-ready-to-burst-bladder-feel.

I think going to the bathroom is often on the female mind. You have either just gone, are thinking of going, or you find yourself in that long lineup waiting to go— you know the one, the one that seems inevitably to be outside of every woman's public bathroom. It really should be your first clue upon entering a building as to where the bathroom is located… you just need to look for the lineup.

Have you ever wondered why it is that there is never a lineup at the men's and there always is at the women's? Is it because there are more women who have to use the bathroom? Is it because women have to remove more clothing? Is it because women have to go in pairs doubling up the number in line? Those who really have to pee and their friends who are along for the ride… or to hold their belongings while they pee… or because they'll have to go eventually… or to hold the door that won't lock...

Finally you locate the bathroom, which is usually the one you find after you've easily found the men's. For some reason men's bathrooms seem to be located first and often in more convenient places. I am sure you've noticed this. It is then you discover that dreaded lineup. Your first thought is often, 'hmmm I should have come earlier… or I did not plan that very well… or I hope they hurry up, I have to go… please don't make me laugh... don't talk to me... my entire focus is on not peeing myself...'

Which brings us to:

When should I get in line?

Questions you need to clarify at this point.

Did you dress in clothing that simplifies the entire process once you enter the stall? Are they lift me ups or pull me downs? Are you in a onesy, you know, the ones that require a complete undress?

How much stuff are you carrying with you? Can you find a place to put all your belongings before you begin the entire process? Will there be a hook on the back of the door or a shelf to put your purse and things, or will you have to somehow juggle it as you go?

Are you going in pairs so someone can hold your stuff while you pee?

Have you been drinking substances like coffee, tea or alcohol? Guess what? They increase the need for speed. You'll feel like you just went and will have to go again.

Have you been doing your Kegel exercises? Have you built up those muscles that are required to pinch off the flow?

Get doing them now... Kegel exercises: A women's guide for how to prepare for the next long lineup.

Want better sex?... Oh wait, we are talking about peeing! Kegel exercises strengthen the pelvic floor muscles, which support all of our organs down there—the uterus, the bladder, the small intestine and the rectum. And they do add to greater sex! You can do Kegel exercises, just about any time.

You may have found your muscles have become weakened through one of the many experiences we have as women. Poor sex... I mean childbirth, pregnancy, holding onto too much, doing too many things at once, and forgetting to go when you need to. And then there is aging... and surgery... and excess weight... and a lack of great sex... Doing Kegel exercises can help lessen or eliminate the leak issue while sneezing, laughing or coughing. It will also allow you to have more control over the muscles that pinch off the flow. Giving you the confidence you need while waiting in that long line up.

How to do Kegel exercises

To get started:

Which muscles are the ones that control your pelvic floor muscles? The next time you are having incredible sex, imagine tightening around... oh wait... that might limit those who learn how to do this. Another method would be to stop urination in midstream. If you succeed, you've got the right muscles. However the sex one is way more fun. Once you've identified your pelvic floor muscles you can do the exercises in any position (oh-oh bring your mind back to the task at hand).

Practice makes perfect. Use your imagination... you are having the most amazing sex and you tighten your pelvic floor muscles, hold the contraction for five seconds, and then relax for five seconds. Try it four or five times in a row. Work up to keeping the muscles contracted for 10 seconds at a time, relaxing for 10 seconds between contractions.

Don't let your mind wander. Which can be hard to do if you are having incredible sex. For best results, focus on tightening only your pelvic floor muscles. Be careful not to flex the muscles in your abdomen, thighs, or buttocks. Avoid holding your breath. Instead, breathe freely during the exercises. Or pant if it is really good!

Repetition is key. Have sex 3 times daily for 30 minutes or more, or, if that is not an option, just do the regular tightening exercises… Aim for at least three sets of 10 repetitions a day.

Make Kegel exercises part of your daily routine and sex too if you want. You can do Kegel exercises discreetly just about any time, whether you're sitting at your desk or relaxing on the couch or having sex. However do not make a habit of doing them while actually peeing as you can stop the bladder from completely emptying and that is bad.

The Six Stage Alert from Your Bladder
Are YOU Listening?

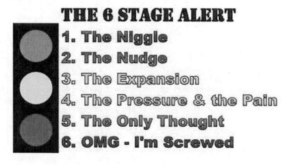

THE 6 STAGE ALERT
1. The Niggle
2. The Nudge
3. The Expansion
4. The Pressure & the Pain
5. The Only Thought
6. OMG - I'm Screwed

1.   **The Niggle**
      There is a niggle from your bladder telling you what is coming… but you still have time. It's like a gentle whisper saying, 'hey, I'm here'.

2. **The Nudge**
There is a nudge, your bladder is telling you that it is starting to fill, you might want to figure out where the bathroom is and start the journey.

3. **The Expansion**
Your bladder is now telling you that it is really time to head to the bathroom as you will need one in the next 5 minutes or less.

4. **The Pressure and Pain**
Your bladder is full but seems to keep stretching putting pressure on your lower belly and your lower back. You feel like it is starting to back up. Are your back teeth floating yet?

5. **The Only Thought**
Where the hell is the bathroom... I need it NOW!

6. **OMG I'm screwed**
I waited too long and there is no way I can move without an accident. Back teeth are definitely floating.

Chapter 2

Does this lineup ever end?

How long will the lineup be?

*A*re you at an event with many people who will all be wanting to use the facility at the same time? You know... when it's half time? when the first band finishes their set? when it's the end of the first period? How many bathrooms are available for the number of women who are in attendance? Oh yeah, you might need to ensure they have not converted some of the women's bathrooms into men's just for that event.

Are you at a shopping mall where they seem to have a better idea of how to plan for women who are shopping and will inevitably need to go the bathroom (they seem to understand that having a lot of bathrooms with a quicker more efficient layout, means less time in line to pee, more time in line to pay = more money)?

Do you have any other issues that increase the need, i.e. a bladder infection, a recent surgery, a weak bladder, a small bladder, a yeast infection, or have the joy of your monthly cycle? All of which means it is going to take longer to do all that needs to be done while in the stall.

Then there are the sporting events, at huge sportsplex, where, oh no, the men were forming line ups for the bathroom. Ah the world is crashing. How can we fix this problem?

Oh I know, let's turn some of the women's bathrooms into men's. Yeah that will fix the problem. In attending this event, you, as a female, will either know or quickly learn where the closest women's bathroom is. You know the quickest path to get to it. The time comes you have to pee. You make your way through the crowds to head to the women's bathroom, grateful there is no lineup. You arrive at the door only to see they have changed it to a men's bathroom. At that moment you are thinking—what the hell is this? And then very quickly, where is another one? I should have come earlier. Your mind is racing as you track down someone who might know where to find the next bathroom. They send you around the entire sportsplex to the other side; you feel the panic build as you wonder if you will make it. Squeezing as tight as you can and yet walking as fast as you can, you hustle around the building to get to the bathroom. Upon arriving you find that looooong U-R-In lineup. As you find your place in line, you pray that you will be able to hold it long enough. You start to do the U-R-In Line Dance—you know the one where you cross, uncross, you shift, you shuffle, you arch, you bend, you do what it is that you can to ease the discomfort you are feeling. You try really hard not to have an accident. You are unaware that the entire line up is moving in a similar fashion to you. Your focus is on staying dry and making it on time.

Did you bring extra supplies?

Sometimes there just is not enough toilet paper for the line up in front of you. What's going to happen when it's your turn?

Do you ignore that niggle?

If you are in public as soon as you get that tiny niggling you need to go, then go, to the bathroom that is. You know you will have to stand in line (well unless you are at a mall that has planned for the occasion).

Then if you get to the front of the line and you really do not have to go yet, you can practice giving up your spot. You'll feel great that you did. You'll allow the person behind you, who has been dancing just trying to hold it in, to go before you. A win/win—you feel great that you could do that and they feel grateful that you did. And if you still do not have to go quite yet, think how many women's day you could make better by allowing them to go first. You know that soon you will have to go.

You are at the front of the line, so you are ready when that really strong urge hits. Now that is preplanning.

If you have a copy of this book in your purse and intend to read while in line, go early, we all know what laughter does to those muscles.

Understanding the basics of how to prevent accidents.

Never bypass a bathroom, always go before you leave home, especially as you age.

Do not laugh when standing in line. We all know laughter is contagious and can be disastrous at the wrong moment.

Do not wear strong perfume as the person next to you might be allergic and it may cause them to sneeze. We know the results of that scenario, don't we?

When you are going to be in a busy place and you know you are going to have to go to the bathroom and wait in line, you might consider wearing a mini pad for that little drop that sneaks out. There is such a selection now—thin dailies, active dailies, sheer dailies, thong dailies, radiant dailies, extra-long dailies, extra-long dailies with fresh scent, dailies unscented, always discreet or they even have 'good bye pads hello Impressa' which is more like a tampon. Then there are the 'Depends' that are dependable pads to take the pressure off.

If you are younger you can hold it longer as long as you don't break the seal. However this is advised against, at least for too long, as it can cause health problems. But that is a whole other book, watch for the sequel.

When you get the niggle that you gotta pee, don't ignore it!

Chapter 3

I gotta pee. I hope this line is moving fast!

Why am I in line again?

You are having way too much fun and time passes without you being aware of it and all of a sudden your body has control of your mind and tells you, you have to go… Now!

You are drinking coffee, tea or alcohol… that results in more frequent urination.

You are attending a workshop, a lecture, or a class and you have to wait for the break to go relieve yourself, just like the hundreds of other women who will be waiting in line with you.

You are at a convention, concert, or sporting event with hundreds or thousands of other women who also have to go. Oh no there is a shortage of women's bathrooms.

You are at a gas station that has one bathroom for both sexes.

You are behind women who love to finish their business and then stand and chat while at the sink or they are putting on their makeup. This creates a backup so no one can move in the narrow space provided.

You wait patiently-impatiently for the woman in front of you, who is in the stall struggling to get her clothes back on and done up before backing up over the toilet so she has room to open the door and exit. The facility you are at has such tiny bathroom stalls that you can barely move around in and there is nowhere to hang a purse. That means it will take women longer in the bathroom.

You are prepared and ready for when the moment hits because you have read the chapter on when to get in line.

You like standing in line.

You are doing market research on what women do while standing in line for the bathroom

It is your moment of solitude away from the demands of the people who came with you.

It is your 'me time'.

The women in front of you have not read this book and missed the education on quick peeing methods.

You have 20 extra copies of our book and you are handing them out while you wait.

Now, let's begin to imagine solutions to the long lineups.

Journey with me through these random thoughts.

We could create separate line-ups for fast peers and slow peers.

Those who are dressed for efficient peeing and not so efficient peeing.

Lines that are dependent on your purpose for being in line… is it number 1 or number 2?

Create a device that women can wear when going out that allows them to stand and pee. They just whip it out and go--no need to back in, no need to undress, no need to undo and pull down or pull up.

Oh yeah, I know why I'm in line... I gotta go pee.

Chapter 4

What to do while in line?

Well, U-R-In Line again. What to do to pass the time until it's your turn?

I am sure you are familiar with the 'In-Line' dance. You know the one! The one where you stand in the hallway waiting to get to the door. You pretend to admire the paintings in the hallway or the design on the carpet or anything but your neighbor, and definitely not the men who waltz past you to get to their bathroom and are back out before you even make it to the door of the women's bathroom!

We could call this the 'U-R-In Line' Shuffle 'cause we are only able to shuffle a few steps forward at a time. Then as you near the door, you feel a sense of relief because you are getting close, only to realize there is a long line inside the bathroom.

Unfortunately, you have started to relax, thinking you were close, and the urgency gets worse! Then it's your turn to hold the door. Someone wants out and it's a narrow doorway. Where to go? How to stand so the lady exiting does not put extra pressure on your bladder? Or heaven forbid, gets you to laugh? You need all your concentration to ensure you make it to a stall. And what if someone has a double length baby carriage going in and someone in a wheelchair wants out? How do you maneuver to give them room, hold the door, hold your bladder, and keep smiling?

But, let us not forget the 'dance'. First, it is a slow walk or shuffle. Then as the line snakes its way closer to those coveted 4 stalls, you start the 'U-R-In Line' Dance—the one where you start to cross your legs without making it too obvious. As time drags on, you don't care who knows, you cross your legs and start to bend slightly at the hips. Then the urgency increases and you start doing cross over steps. Movement at this point could be dangerous, but you have to keep moving forward. You must reach one of those four stalls soon!

U-R-In Line Song/Ditty

One way to pass the time is to sing the 'U-R-In Line'
song/ditty:

> I'm on my way
> I'm on my way
> I'm in line again
> I'm on my way
> I gotta pee!
> I'm on my way
> If only I'd stopped 5 back
> I'm on my way
> Get outta my way
> I gotta pee!

U-R-In Line Dance

You could also do the U-R-In Line dance:

> Step, step, step
> Shuffle, shuffle
> Step, pause
> Step, pause
> Shuffle, shuffle
> Turn with back to the wall
> Squeeze tight
> Side step, side step
> Smile
> Face forward again
> Shuffle, shuffle
> Cross legs

Step, step
Cross legs the other way
Step, step
Shuffle, shuffle
Cross legs
Bend hips
Cross-over step, step
Run for the stall.

Chapter 5

Careful...
Laughter

may cause tears
of another kind!

The Things That Can Cause Accidents While U-R-In Line

Have you ever felt that first niggle of having to go, but you ignored it? Have you ever ignored it to the point that you could barely move? God forbid there might be a lineup! This is where the U-R-In Line dance becomes motionless. Legs are crossed, hips are bent, all muscles in the pelvic area are tensed and contracted.

You know the pose.

If this is your state when you get in line, then there are certain things you really want to avoid. The first thing you want to avoid is anything that will cause a physical reaction—it is taking all of your attention to keep the 'tears' from running down your legs. Laughter is the next no-no. Laughter causes you to tighten and relax muscles that are a necessity to staying dry and dangerous if relaxed at the wrong time. The third thing to avoid is jostling of any kind. Any movement or extra pressure on your body, may cause you to have 'tears' run down your legs. This is to be avoided at all costs!

So if you see a sister doing this form of the U-R-In Line dance, please, please, please, have compassion and allow her to go first.

On another note, once you have completed the U-R-In Line dance, be courteous to those still performing the dance and move out of the way. Allow those still dancing, the freedom to move as they need, with lots of space. You know you'll be back in the dance soon enough.

Here are some simple calming and relaxation exercises.

Okay we only want you to relax to a point. Really these are just distractions to help you forget what is going on in your body and the current situation you find yourself in.

1. Take a few deep breaths but not too deep, we don't want to add pressure
2. Do the butterfly exercise — tap on the opposite thigh with your fingertips. That is if you have free hands.
3. Definitely make sure that you are doing gentle Kegels to hold all that flow back.
4. Talk to your neighbor. You'll discover you are not alone in how you feel and it will distract you.
5. Sing the U-R-In Line Ditty — but not too loud as you'll make others laugh and we know what that causes.

Don't worry your turn will come... so... oo... n... ish!

Chapter 6

"So is the line moving
very fast?"

Get to Know Your Neighbor

If you are middle aged or grew up in a small town, you may remember a time when you knew everyone on your street or in your entire town!

Well, waiting in line is a perfect time to rekindle the lost art of getting to know your neighbor.

Why is it that we don't speak to our neighbor in a line up? Who decided that we can't build community while waiting? It's time to build a community again, one line up or one pee at a time.

Start a conversation.

Here are a few suggestions:
·   Can you believe it? We're in line again.
·   Been here often?
·   Is this the fast lane?
·   Look how the engineers and architects are helping us build community—only 5 stalls for 500 women.

Another way to form community is to recognize the urgency of the U-R-In Line dance. If you're next in line for a stall and the woman behind you is urgently doing the dance and you're not, consider letting her go ahead of you. Beware of imitators though—they may try to take advantage of your generosity.

What will you discuss?

Chances are you are at the same affair so you could ask how they are enjoying the event. And if they're not at the same one, ask what they are attending and how is it. Become curious and interested in the other person. It makes the time go wa-aaaa-aaa-yy faster and it takes your mind off having to go pee.

If you're not in line or you have just finished with the U-R-In Line dance, encourage your sisters that they can make it, that you believe in them. You know they have it in them to make it safely to the stall. And to keep the focus!

Seriously though, let's acknowledge each other in line—smile and say hello.

Chapter 7

Don't worry...
I'll save You!

I'm Finally In

Once the stall door finally opens there is the moment of 'thank goodness'. You try to be patient while the person makes their way out of the bathroom with all of their stuff and makes their way slowly through the narrow passage of those women entering and those leaving the bathroom stalls. When you see your opening, you dash to the stall. The only thought at this point, is that there will be a sense of relief soon. Once you get in, you turn sideways, sometimes having to stand beside or straddle the toilet to get the door closed. You finally close it, praying that it will lock. Sometimes it does and sometimes it doesn't. When it doesn't you have to add a whole new skill to your skill set—remove the necessary clothes, keep the door closed, sit down and pee and finish your job, all at the same time.

Let's say for this instance you don't have to worry that the door locks. Yay. Then you look for that hook on the back of the door or on occasion on the sidewall. This hook is as important as the lock on the door or toilet paper. This hook means that you do not have to put your purse/bag on the floor. Because unless that floor is being mopped every five minutes, odds are it is pretty disgusting. But sometimes you do not have any other options, although you can try to hold onto your bag while doing all the fun stuff, like pulling up your shirt and getting your pants down, in that narrow environment just so you can sit down and pee.

The key once you are in, is to do your job quickly. You try to lock the door, find where to put your bag, then rearrange your clothes—which can mean undo belts, buttons, zippers and/or pull up jackets, shirts, dresses and then pull down pants, leggings, underwear. Whew, you haven't even got to the actual job and it's already exhausting.

But what if the door doesn't lock?

I'm sure you know that is never fun. If you've followed the unwritten code and taken another woman with you, then you have someone to hold it. If you haven't then you have to get creative. Now the question is can you stretch enough while sitting so that your hand will keep the door closed? Or at least mostly closed? Another trick many women have learned to master—you sit, shifting forward as far as you can, hold your clothes with one hand (when needed), and reach out with the other, holding the door closed. Or you have your hands full, so you stretch one leg out to keep the door closed while you sit. Then when you are finished and need to stand up, well you really need both hands to pull up, zip up, and rearrange clothes and you need your legs to stand. What to do? Do you let go of the door? Do you use your head to keep it closed? Or do you turn and rest your shoulder against it while you get dressed?

It is a bit of a conundrum.

The Art of the Pee.

Going pee isn't as easy as it sounds… at least not in public. We've talked about all that you're wearing that has to be moved or removed just so you can sit but the question is do you sit?

Now some ladies do not have an issue with sitting on a public toilet seat while other women do.

If you are overly concerned about germs—although at this point, there is no point—put three sheets of toilet paper on each side of the toilet seat. That should give you some security. If you are really concerned, be sure to carry those paper seat covers with you.

But I don't want to sit.

It's one thing to shift and lift and drop just so you can sit down on the toilet but if you will not sit on the toilet, that takes a whole new set of skills. Now you have to adjust everything, hold your clothes in place so they don't fall and then really work your hip and thigh muscles to keep you delicately balanced while hovering over the toilet. And you have to make sure that your aim is good. The last thing you want is to accidently pee on your leg. Ew! But it happens.

Before you leave, if you haven't lifted the toilet seat before hovering, please be sure to wipe it off so it's clean and dry for the next person.

Really, it's quite a talent. Sometimes it is a must, hovering just above that toilet seat, keeping a safe distance between that grungy seat and your bare ass.

Just try not to take a lot of time. There are a lot of women still waiting to get in. But no pressure.

The good news is that you will have done some really good strengthening and endurance exercises.

What about the noise?

Something you have to know, is that we all make noises when we go to the bathroom. Unfortunately, we all tend to be quite embarrassed by them. In fact, I bet you pray that it won't be one of those moments where you do make a lot of noise. The truth is that we tinkle, we dribble, we spurt, it's intermittent, we spray, we pee like it is a waterfall that doesn't sound like it will ever end. Sometimes we fart—anywhere from toots to rippers to outright explosions. It may sound awful but it sure feels good. And then there is number two. We plop, we drop, and we have explosions. We grunt, we groan, we sigh with relief. The truth is that going to the bathroom isn't pretty or all that quiet, but it is normal.

Maybe we should be more like men. We should have peeing competitions—see how far we can pee or how high. That might not be such a good idea for us... but we can see who can pee the fastest... who can pee the loudest... who can create the best tune...

Nobody wants it to be that way or to have others hear them but it is a fact. One that we just need to accept. It can sound super loud to you but don't worry every woman feels for you as they have all been there and on that day, in that public bathroom, they pray it won't be them. We spend too much time being embarrassed by something that is natural and is extremely important to our health.

Let's stop feeling bad about what we do… it's just nature.

What's the right amount of toilet paper and how do you fold it?

Now that you are finished doing your job, wipe. But the question is what is the right amount of toilet paper? What is too much? Do you fold or crumple it up? It really doesn't matter how you organize your toilet paper, just remember it is about not wasting time. But don't use twelve sheets and then use a second bunch of twelve. Three or four is plenty and for those messy moments, use a second bunch. You really don't need to use a ton of paper.

The rolls don't get replaced often enough so this is another reason why it is good to always carry supplies with you—a tissue always works well. And don't be shy to ask your neighbor for some. We've all been there when there is no toilet paper and we have no supplies. Ugh. Not fun.

Be sure to flush when you are finished. Don't leave your leavings for someone else to deal with. If the toilet is broken, be sure to tell the next person in line and be sure to tell a staff from the venue so they can get it fixed. If you happen to get into a stall that hasn't been flushed, take a second and flush it first. You might have to hold down the handle for a few seconds to get it to flush properly. Not all public bathrooms are created equally and not all toilets function properly.

If you are having your menstrual cycle, wrap your tampon or pad in a toilet paper and put it in the container provided for it. Do not put your pad or tampon in the toilet, it can and often does, plug it. That means another toilet is out of commission which guarantees longer wait times for the women in line.

You have to pee and you have to poo,

It is just a fact you have to do.

Try not to let the nerves or the worry of going to the bathroom bother you. For some people though it is a major issue, to the point they will do everything to avoid public bathrooms. Especially busy ones. Be aware that for some it is really stressful.

Now that you are finished,
   Pull up
   Zip up
   And hustle out
   Keep the line moving…

You can fix all of your clothes once out of the stall. Besides you'll have a tiny bit more space.

Every time you enter a stall be sure to look for the following:
- does the door lock
- is there a hook
- is there toilet paper
- has it been flushed
- is there spray on the seat — wipe it first.

And if you are in the sixth stage of alert none of this matters, just move your clothing and get the relief you are seeking. That really is the only thing that is important at this stage. We do want to prevent an accident.

Chapter 8

Beyond Relief... *Whew! Made it in time!*

After the Pee - Aaaaahhhh

Does this sound familiar?

There is no greater relief than when you are finished. Aaaahhh. It feels so good and is almost a moment to savor. But then you start to think, where is the toilet paper? Is there any toilet paper? Now in some cases the toilet paper dispenser is so large it should almost never need to be refilled but when you are in there, it feels like it never actually has been. It almost always seems to be out of paper. How can it be out when it's so large? And you know it's there because you've probably whacked your elbow on it or had to shift to the other side as it won't let you sit properly on the toilet. In other bathrooms, you're looking for the normal size dispenser, usually at the back of your elbow. You have to twist yourself like a pretzel to get to it. You finally get to finish. The relief is so welcome you want to take a moment to breathe a sigh of relief… however, there is no time for that. Women are waiting. And most are in as much discomfort as you were. So be kind and once you are done, do your best to pull up, zip up, pull down, grab your stuff and exit the bathroom stall so that the next woman can feel the same relief that you are now experiencing.

Exiting the Stall

After you pee, you know someone is waiting for your stall, so you rush to get out. But be careful, it is a busy area, there are other women entering and exiting others as well. Determined to get out of there, you make your way to the sink. Unfortunately you might have to stand in another lineup. Although this one is usually only 2 or 3 deep.

There usually isn't that much space, so the lineup coming in gets jostled by the lineup trying to reach the sinks and then get out of the bathroom. It makes it awkward for those trying to get to the sink to wash their hands. When bathrooms are designed well, the sinks are away from the stalls and aren't impacted by the lineup still trying to come in.

Washing your hands.

When you do get to the counter, do not lean against it, odds are it is wet. The counter tends to get very splashed with water. You have to be careful or the front of your pants will get wet and then people will think you peed yourself. Something you just spent the last fifteen minutes trying to prevent.

You reach for the soap and hardly any spurts out, so you wash with what you have and rinse your hands under what is often cold water. Then you go to the blow dryer only to get a really weak blow job. You shake your hands to finish drying them. If they have hand dryers, use them but unless there is a really good one with lots of pressure, you won't have time to dry your hands fully.

What is the right amount of paper towel? Like toilet paper, people seem to think they need 3, 4 or 5 to dry their hands. Really one will do the job, two if you must. Again the more each of us respects the supplies, the more there will be for those who follow us. Never mind that it truly does help Mother Nature when we don't overuse or abuse those things we produce to make our lives simpler.

After you've washed your hands, presuming there is soap, and after you've dried your hands, presuming there are paper towels, use the paper towel to wipe the counter. It may save someone else some embarrassment.

Be kind to those still in line.

Women love to primp and fix their hair and makeup, which is great. For the sake of bladder pain, please be kind and try to hurry and move out of the way and exit the bathroom. Bathrooms are very crowded and women are focused on having to pee and get some relief.

Chatting is a great thing to be doing, however when you are no longer in the lineup to go to the bathroom, please take your conversation outside the women's bathroom. There just isn't room to accommodate you along with those in line entering the bathroom and those trying to wash their hands and leave. In those rare cases where space is provided, use this space to fix your make-up, hair and have your conversation but keep the line moving. If it gets too crowded please finish up and head out so that those who've just finished and those still doing the U-R-In line dance have some space.

Going to a public bathroom can be major issue.

For some people going to a public bathroom is quite an ordeal. They are not comfortable with peeing in public and find it quite stressful. For others they find it quite claustrophobic. So be aware that the woman who is hurrying to get out as much as she got in, may not be comfortable there at all.

Be respectful... Keep it moving...

Chapter 9

So, how does this thing flush?

T**he Not so Automatic, Automatic Bathroom But it Says It's Automatic!**

In today's world of germs and germ phobia, everything is automatic so we don't actually have to touch anything. We have automatic flushing toilets. Automatic water taps. Automatic soap dispensers. Automatic dryers. Automatic towel dispensers. Automatic lights. Automatic garbage can lids. There are even toilets that have automatic lid lifters!

Now-a-days, the only thing that is not automatic is the opening and closing of the bathroom stall door, the locking of the stall door, or helping you arrange your clothes (which is probably a good thing).

Getting the toilet to flush.

The only challenge with all this automaticity is that it isn't always automatic. You know the scene. You finished going to the bathroom, you are arranging your clothes, you finish arranging your clothes and the toilet still hasn't flushed. So you say to yourself, 'okay, no problem, I'll just flush it manually'. Then you look for how you might do that. There is no handle to push down. There is no tank on the back of the toilet, so nothing to push there. Is there a button near the 'not working' automatic sensor? No, not there either. Ok, so where can it be? Meanwhile you are starting to feel guilty because you're taking so long in the stall, but you don't want to leave your 'leavings' for the next person, so you look around the bowl of the toilet — nothing there. Then you look around the base of the toilet and you see a lever, waaaay back against the wall. You then wonder how the heck you're supposed to reach it. You maneuver you and your bags so you can stick a leg between the bowl and the stall wall so you can just reach the lever with your foot. You touch the lever. Nothing happens. You press harder. Finally, it flushes! You feel like cheering, but you still have to get out so the next person can get in. As a courtesy, tell the next in line about the foot pedal so they are quicker.

And then there are the toilets that flush every 10 seconds whether needed or not. These are the ones that then require you to use extra toilet paper to dry off.

The soap, sink and drying your hands.

You finally get past the automatic flush to get to the next automatic devices—the water and the soap. This could be considered another form of dance, but with the hands. You place your hand in front of the sensor for the taps—nothing. You wave your hand—still nothing. You then try the other hand, thinking maybe the sensor is sensitive to either left or right hands—still nothing. You then try rubbing the sensor—still nothing. In frustration, you really start waving and are just about to try another sink, when, hallelujah, the water starts coming out of the tap. And then the pressure is so great, the water is splashing everywhere! No wonder, there is water all over the counter. You try to block the spray of water while trying to get some soap. Another 'dance' ensues.

Or, you reach for the soap first, you get a big dollop, then to put your hands under the tap but no water comes out. You then go through the above 'dance' trying to get water and not lose your soap or spread the soap everywhere.

You finally get your hands washed, only to go to the automatic towel dispenser to find:

a) it is empty,
b) it is stuck or
c) it gives you a piece of paper the size of a square of toilet paper.

You wave your hand in front of the sensor to get more paper and nothing. You look for a lever to push or a dial to turn to get more paper—nothing. Now what? You wave your hand in front of the sensor, nice and slow. Still nothing. You begin to wonder if you are supposed to sing to it or something like that. Maybe it is face recognition and you're supposed to put your face in front of the sensor. Nope. That didn't work either. You try waving one more time, this time really slowly, and it won't stop! There is paper everywhere! So much for conserving!

And what about those automatic air dryers? You get ones that barely blow to ones that blow so hard, they ripple your skin. You get ones that blow cold air, ones that blow warm air, and even some that blow hot air—and not just the kind of hot air that some people blow. You get blow dryers that let you drip all over the floor. Ones that actually blow enough air to dry your hands without too much drip. And then you get the Cadillac version—the ones that you put your hands into so the water drips into the machine, not on the floor, and it dries your hands within seconds. If we're going to have a blow job, it might as well be a good one!

So as you head off to join the line-up once again, you now have just one more thing to add to your list of worries of using a public bathroom — is it automatic, semi-automatic or...? Will it work? What do I do if it doesn't?

And men wonder why we take so long!?!

Chapter 10

Hmm...
Does
size matter?

Size Does Matter!

Of the stall that is. Have you ever stood in line watching those coveted doors opening and closing, only to realize that one of them opens out, and it isn't the wheelchair accessible stall? As you watch this stall, you begin to realize that something is different—something is not good. Then you begin to hope that you don't get that stall. However it seems that what you think about comes about. Guess which stall you get! As you walk slowly towards the dreaded stall, hoping another door will open on your way, you get to the stall with the door that opens out, to find a tiny stall. You've heard of tiny homes? Well, I am sure this is where they got the concept.

As you look at this stall, knowing that you are holding up the line, you are trying to decide how best to enter the stall with all your stuff. And heaven forbid if you are a voluptuous woman! You decide that the best way to enter is backward because there is no room to maneuver in there—thus why the door opens outwards. So you back in, stand over the toilet, close the door, then you attempt to pull up or down without banging against the walls or door. You finally get ready and you sit, only to realize that with the backpack and large purse, you cannot sit all the way back because of the wall, but you cannot sit too far forward because of the door. You persevere and get sat, sort of, only to finish and wonder where the toilet paper is. Oh there it is, at the end of your nose on the back of the door! Right about now, you are wishing the wheelchair stall had been open instead.

Let's talk about Wheelchairs.

Speaking of wheelchair stalls, let's talk about the older wheelchair accessible stalls. They used to be built to a certain specification, but whoever specified the size, obviously did not use a wheelchair. The stalls were built so that the wheelchair and the person would fit, but not in a way that would allow the person to close the door and then transfer to the toilet. The space for the wheelchair was beside the toilet, but not in a position that was conducive to transferring to the toilet; especially with those grab bars they used to install by toilets to 'aid' people in remaining safe while on the toilet. And just imagine if that person in the wheelchair has someone come in to help them onto or off the toilet? There is no room for an extra person.

I keep thinking that we need to find the designer and put them in a wheelchair, tie their legs so they can't use them, put a backpack on their back, with a large purse over one shoulder, then let them maneuver into a woman's bathroom and see how they fair.

What if it's not a dream?

I have had this recurring dream/nightmare, where I get to this Tiny Stall, only to discover that it is so tiny, a real toilet does not even fit! What they have is a hole in the floor, with this white tube-like thing propped against the wall. As you stand there looking at it, a shot of water sprays up into the air – oh great, a self-flushing 'Tiny Toilet'. You have to pull the 'toilet' to cover the hole, then back out of the stall only to back into the stall, close the door and hope that the 'toilet' is still propped over the hole in the floor. Because the toilet is hinged, it does not stay over the hole, so you must somehow hold the toilet in place, close the door, move your clothing and… Then you sit precariously on this

Tiny Toilet and see a floor drain right in front of you. When another toilet flushes, the water in the drain, sprays up right in your face. You quickly grab toilet paper to cover your face and block most of the water, but the spray is so fine, it gets past your hands. Now that you are finished, and the 'Tiny Toilet' has flushed and gotten you all wet, you must stand up carefully because you know the toilet is moving back against the wall leaving a hole in the middle of the floor with water sporadically spraying upwards. You still need to rearrange your clothes, keep them dry and get out of the stall without stepping in anything!

I just hope that no architect or designer of women's bathrooms ever reads this and gets an idea!

I am a fairly small woman so I can maneuver somewhat in these stalls, but what of our beautiful sisters who are voluptuous. How do they manage?

Whoever thought up the design of these stalls was only thinking of it from a space perspective and not a human perspective. I think it is time we added the human perspective back in!

Chapter 11

Going pee can get complicated

Complications of going to the bathroom.

Are you having so much fun you laugh a lot?

Are you feeling a cold coming on, or have allergies that may cause you to sneeze?

Age is a factor, are you young and strong, and all your muscles hold tight, or have you a child or two, over the years those necessary muscles do not tighten as much?

Are you just there to pee or did your body decide, 'ya I don't care that we're out in public, I need to get rid of that food that I just ate. Here I'll give you a whiff!'

So you finally make it to the bathroom door only to see how narrow the space is between the lineup coming in and the lineup exiting. You have your luggage in tow as well as that big purse and a small child. How are you going to manage? You squeeze by the other women as they leave and make your way into the stall. What were they thinking putting in such tiny stalls? You will never fit, you will have to wait for the handicapped stall to become available… but you really, really have to go. There is just no way you can fit. You give up your spot in line to those waiting behind you until the handicap stall opens up. At that moment you dash for it and quickly close the door and sit, or do you sit… Oh yay, the seat is wet. Do you cover it with toilet paper? Or take that stance of hovering just above the seat? At this point you just want relief.

What if women have more going on for them.

At this moment you think of the other women in line and wonder how they would manage if they have bladder issues? a bladder infection? or god forbid they are 9 months pregnant? or worse have diarrhea? or they have their period and they have waited too long between changes? The flow is too heavy. They should have come an hour ago to take care of business.

As you finish your business you exit the stall and look at the women in line, and you notice what some of their challenges are—an elderly lady with a walker; a woman with a cane; a woman pushing a carriage and she's wearing a backpack; a woman who has been drinking and is a little inebriated, who obviously really has to go; a woman on crutches with a full leg cast and a backpack, wow you can feel for her. As you observe the women in line, you realize how women always multitask, except when they are standing in line to pee. There is no multi-tasking, well, other than managing to maneuver that luggage and backpack and child all the while tightening those Kegels and doing the U-R-In-Line Dance.

Oh the joys of being a woman!

Chapter 12

It's almost perfect!

The Perfect Public Bathroom for Women

Public bathrooms often do not have a lot of thought going into them. Although we will say that more modern malls have done a good job at trying to make the bathrooms more appealing and user friendly.

So what would the perfect women's public bathroom look like?

Great question.

It would be made of marble, with each bathroom being an individual bathroom, like one would have at home (minus the tub or shower of course). There would be a chair to set down any bags/purses/backpacks/luggage/jackets/other belongings. There would be space so that when you open the door you actually have to cross the room to reach the toilet. It would be painted in bright, warm, welcoming colors. Soft music would be playing in the background. Fresh scented healthy essential oils would keep the room at an optimal nice smell. For those who are sensitive there would be the option to have unscented. The toilet seat would be soft yet firm. There would be a bidet. When a woman is finished her job, water gently washes her privates, while sitting on the toilet and then there is an air blower to dry her—should she choose to use it. Toilet paper so soft it feels like soft fluffy, velvet. The sink would be a clam shape sitting on top of an antique dresser. There would be an array of natural soaps and scents from no smell to lavender, jasmine…

Oh did I mention there would be a sink in each bathroom?

The bathroom would be its own closed off room so that women wouldn't have to worry about being heard when they pee or poo. And the music would soothe any stressed nerves.

A masseuse would also be fabulous to ensure that our muscles and body are relaxed so that we can enjoy the rest of the event we are attending. But we do understand that might be a little over the top.

Now this would be amazing but highly unlikely and that's okay, we get it, however there are a few things that really are kind of essential. Truly we aren't asking for much just enough so that when we know we are going to an event with lots of other women, we won't have to be so concerned about the lineup that we know we will encounter with the women's bathroom.

After all men and women are not created the same.

This is what we would truly appreciate:

1. Stalls big enough you can turn around in.

2. Hooks to hang stuff on.

3. Secure toilet seats, so they don't shoot off when you sit down.

4. A lock that works.

5. Enough stalls so that the lineup isn't more than 10 minutes to get into the toilet.

6. Sinks set away from the toilets so that the two lineups—those entering, those waiting, and those trying to wash their hands—aren't bumping into each other and squeezing past each other.

7. Toilet paper that could not be used as sanding paper and there is an endless supply of it.

8. Blow dryers that actually work and dry hands within seconds.

9. And/or paper towels that are big enough to wipe hands on, are absorbent, and there is an endless supply of them.

10. Some air flow, not cold but so that the bathrooms aren't so stuffy.

11. Filtered air so that smells are soon sucked out and fresh air is circulated in.

It might even be an idea to have an enter and exit doorway. Enter near the bathroom stalls and then walk the opposite direction to wash hands and exit through another door. That way women don't have to squish by the still-waiting-in-line-to-pee-women.

What we really want is for those who create public bathrooms and host events to take a little more time to take into consideration what women have to go through. Especially when there are going to be events where you are guaranteed to stand in bathroom lineups.

It might be a surprise but women do attend events so that they can actually see and enjoy the event and not spend their time standing in the U-R-In line waiting to pee.

The truth is that you make a woman happy, she will not only be back to your venue but will bring friends. Upset a woman with the issue of the bathrooms and she will not come back and she will tell others.

The End

$\mathcal{Y}$ou attend an event, excited to be there. You paid good money for it, you want to have fun, to get a break from your normal life, to meet others, to learn… but then you have to go pee. And that's when it hits you, you'll be standing in line.

It is a process to have to pee in public bathrooms.
    Where is the bathroom?
    How long does it take to get there?
    How long will you be in line?
    How bad do you have to go?
    When do you get in line?

Did you do your Kegels in the last 10 or 20 years?

Will you be able to turn around when in the stall?

Will the door lock?

Is there a hook or someplace to put your belongings?

Is there toilet paper?

Is the seat wet?

How do you flush the toilet?

And sadly the knowledge that when you are finished the relief is short lived because you know you will be in line again… soon…

BUT! You're not alone.

There are a few guarantees in life—you live, you die, and if you're a woman, you will stand in a lineup waiting to enter a tiny, public bathroom stall to go pee.

There are so many ups and downs in life often with many challenges and it's often easy to forget the good moments. Life can be stressful and you may feel you are often alone. We want to change that. We want women to know they are there for each other. It's a matter of knowing we're all in this stall, bathroom stall that is, together.

It's what we make of it that matters.

Standing in line is never fun. In fact it can be downright painful at times. Every woman has been in the U-R-In Line, you know standing in line for the women's public bathroom. It's almost a rite of passage. Needless to say every woman has experienced a very uncomfortable bladder and maybe even an accident or two. We don't want that to happen to anyone. So the next time you are standing in the U-R-In Line, let's remove some of the stress—talk to your neighbor, sing the U-R-In Line Ditty, do the U-R-In Line Dance. You just never know how long you'll be hanging out there, so you might as well make the most of it. Your neighbor just might become your new best friend. Or at least one who gets what you're going through. And this will help to distract you from the discomfort you're feeling.

Let's pull it together ladies and be there for each other. Women thrive in community! It's who we are. Remember this the next time you're in the U-R-In line. Be sure to sing our ditty, to dance, and to say hello to your dance partners.

Live… Love… Laugh… just don't laugh too hard while you are in the lineup for the public bathroom. Accidents are not our goal.

We're in the U-R-In Line together ladies. Let's make the most of it.

Let's just
bring our
own!

Thank you for reading

Don't Laugh

A Woman's Playbook to in the U-R-In Line for the Women's Public Bathroom... Again.

We hope you enjoyed reading it as much as we enjoyed writing it.

Please review it, it helps others to find it.

Recommend it to family and friends, coworkers, women and men everywhere. Let them have a good laugh as well.

You can connect with us on **Facebook –**

Where Women Gather

Email us at: wherefemalesgather@gmail.com

About the Authors

Alisa Gamblin

    Alisa Gamblin is a certified hypnotherapist, sound and energy healer, public speaker, workshop facilitator, world traveler and writer. Her writing career began in detention in grade 4—her 1st 2000 word essay. Even then her creative mind found writing came as a natural ability, which allowed her to share a message. Alisa now uses her natural writing abilities to craft stories that hold deeper meaning and secrets to creating a better life. Her passion and purpose is awakening women, around the globe, to their greatness.

Learn more at www.thebeliefconnection.com